It's Your Time to Shine

Lynette Hagin

FAITH LIBRARY PUBLICATIONS®

30 29 28 27 26 25 24 08 07 06 05 04 03 02

It's Your Time to Shine
ISBN-13: 978-0-89276-805-9
ISBN-10: 0-89276-805-3

Printed in the USA

In the U.S. write:
Kenneth Hagin Ministries
P.O. Box 50126
Tulsa, OK 74150-0126
1-888-28-FAITH
www.rhema.org

In Canada write:
Kenneth Hagin Ministries
P.O. Box 231
Schomberg, Ontario
Canada L0G 1T0
1-866-70-RHEMA
www.rhemacanada.org

Contents

Introduction v

1. **A New Candle** (Keeping the Sparkle in Your Life) 1

   Arise, shine; For your light has come! And the glory of the Lord is risen upon you.—Isaiah 60:1 (NKJV)

2. **A New Toothbrush** (Cleaning Up the Words of Your Mouth) 19

   You will also declare a thing, And it will be established for you; So light will shine on your ways.—Job 22:28 (NKJV)

3. **A New Fragrance** (Living God's Way—the Act of Walking in Love) 37

   But the path of the just is like the shining sun, That shines ever brighter unto the perfect day.—Proverbs 4:18 (NKJV)

4. **A New Garment** (Putting Into Practice the Power of Praise) 55

   God be merciful to us and bless us, And cause His face to shine upon us.—Psalm 67:1 (NKJV)

Conclusion 67

Notes 69

Introduction

I have hundreds of bags. They are my weakness. If there's a free bag offered at a store, I will go and buy the make-up or other product being offered so I'll get the free bag. Whether I need the make-up or not, I have to have the free bag, especially if it is different than the others I already have. I love bags!

One bag that I've had for a long time looks all wrinkled and worn-out. I've spilled things in it and taken it on airplanes so often that it just looks tired and weary and not quite as shiny as it used to be. Life can make us feel that way sometimes too. We can become tired and weary and tarnished (emotionally), just like that old bag of mine. Yet that's not how God wants us to live.

The world around us seems to be rocking at times, and this keeps many people down, worried, stressed, and panicky. Even many Christians have lost their luster for life and their joy has turned into fear. Their lives have become nothing more than a tarnished, hard, and burdensome existence. Before writing this book I thought about why people experience this and what they can do to change this situation. I believe the Lord showed me the answers to these questions through an object lesson involving four common, ordinary items we often have around us.

The title, *It's Your Time to Shine,* reveals the most important message I want to share with you in this book. Since we are human and living "in" this world, our spiritual varnish often becomes tarnished and dull by the cares of this life. But just as we would put away our tattered and torn garments in exchange for new ones, God desires that we continue to apply new coats of polish and sheen to our lives by constantly putting on the garment of praise.

ISAIAH 61:3

3 . . . Give unto them . . . the garment of praise for the spirit of heaviness . . . that [the Lord] might be glorified.

Putting on the garment of praise is what lifts our spirits and keeps us shining and filled with the joy of the Lord. The decision to praise God in good times and bad can cause us to deal with the pressures, stresses, failures, and successes of everyday life with ease.

Our vehicles do not automatically sparkle and shine. My husband, son, and some of my grandsons are into cars, motorcycles, and racing. Those vehicles get pretty filthy and dirty during practice runs, repairs, and maintenance. But when race day comes and when the car or motorcycle is driven to the pit area or starting line, you almost have to shake your head to believe that it is the same vehicle it was just the day before. It has been washed, scrubbed, detailed, and waxed. The vehicle is now brilliant and shiny—ready and prepared for the race!

Likewise, if we're having a trying day and we put on a brand-new garment in the natural, it can change how we feel for the better. How much more will we change and shine as putting on this garment of praise polishes us up? It can change our outlook because it draws us closer to God. It brings us into His Presence and makes us want to open our hearts and commit every area of our lives to Him; and it makes us want to desire that His will be done in and through us. When we have that kind of desire, the Lord will lead us, guide us, minister to us, and shine through us in a great and mighty way!

Chapter 1

A New Candle

Keeping the Sparkle in Your Life

PROVERBS 20:27

27 The spirit of man is the candle of the Lord, searching all the inward parts of the belly.

One time my daughter, Denise, came over to visit and I had every candle in the house lit. She looked around and said, "Mom, are you having a bad day?"

"I needed my candles today," I told her, and she had felt the same way herself.

"Mom, I had all the candles in my house lit too," she replied.

We both have fun with candles and love to buy new ones for each other. When we first take a candle out of our bag, that candle is beautiful. It smells wonderful, and it burns with a beautiful flame. But after about a month of use, it doesn't look good or burn well anymore. The wax is almost melted down to the bottom, the light's just about gone out, the fragrance is weak, and there's soot on what's left of the candle.

In the days in which we are living, we can become like that candle when all the cares of life start overtaking us. Our light can be almost extinguished, and we can feel as if we're worn down to the very bottom.

So many people try to figure out the solution to their problems on their own; or they just want to hear what they can do to be a success so they can heap blessings on themselves. However, the most important thing we need to know is something that my mom and dad indelibly impressed upon me early in life.

MATTHEW 6:33

33 Seek ye first the kingdom of God, and his righteousness; and all these things shall be added unto you.

If we're not careful, we can become so concerned about seeking things that we forget about seeking the One who is able to give us those things. My parents taught me the top priority. They said, "Lynette, as long as you will put seeking God's kingdom first, you won't have to worry about anything else in life because the blessings will overtake you."

First Corinthians 2:9 says, "*No eye has seen, no ear has heard, no mind has conceived what God has prepared for those who love him*" (NIV 1984). Every time I read this scripture it gets stronger on the inside of me, and the next verse says, "*but God has revealed it to us by his Spirit*." How are we going to find out what God has prepared for those of us who love Him? *By His Spirit!*

Many Christians have gotten away from seeking first the kingdom of God. They've become distracted by "the Martha syndrome," which is described in Luke 10. Martha was trying to work everything out in her own wisdom and strength, but her sister, Mary, "*sat at the Lord's feet listening to what he said*" (v. 39 NIV 1984). What did Jesus tell Martha when she began to complain about her sister's lack of help in serving their guests? "*You are worried and upset about many things, but only one thing is needed. Mary has chosen what is better, and it will not be taken away from her*" (vv. 41–42 NIV 1984).

Now certainly work must be accomplished, but in the midst of doing the work that needs to be done, we must recognize the importance and value of Mary's choice. We must learn to bask in the Presence of the Lord as she did. Otherwise, we neglect the very tool that will enable us to make right decisions and perform our tasks easily—communion with our Heavenly Father.

You see, if Satan knows that he can't get us to stop serving the Lord, that he can't throw us off course that way, he'll try to keep us busy doing natural things. Now, we certainly must do some of those things, but often we find ourselves becoming busier and busier in the natural things of this world. That can even involve doing good things for God, yet it's keeping us from what's most important for us to do—reading God's Word, talking to Him daily, and getting to know Him personally. These are the things that will help us get where we need to go in life.

Many of us go to every seminar that we can on time management. Then we start working on our "to do" list. Then we check off our "missions accomplished," or our tasks completed. We can be so focused on our agenda that we forget to ask God, "What is Your agenda for this day, Lord?"

I want to ask you a question. Would God be pleased with your agenda? On your "to do" list does it say, "Pray. Read the Bible. Worship the Lord."? If not, don't feel condemned. Most of our "to do" lists say, "Go to a meeting. Go to the store. Pick up this. Do that." But we forget to include, "Worship the Lord and let Him speak to me." We'll talk more about worship later, but when we worship God, it creates an atmosphere that is conducive to prayer, one where we can hear from and be led by the Lord.

Keep the Light Burning

When we go to God in prayer, we commune with Him, and that's the time He speaks to our hearts. "*Draw near to God, and He will draw near to you*" (James 4:8 HCSB). Otherwise, we will go around in circles because we aren't listening to His voice. His voice will be very faint and we'll end up becoming encompassed with all the cares in life that cause our lights to fade.

We know that we were washed in the precious blood of Jesus (if we've received Him as our Lord and Savior) and that He paid the price for our salvation and for our healing. But when our sanctification level starts getting a little low, soon some of the old thoughts come up again.

If we get attacked with sickness, for instance, we forget that Jesus paid the price for our healing when He bore the stripes on His back at the same time that He bore our sins. So our light goes dim because we've forgotten what the Lord did for us on the cross.

Or we may be fighting a battle and standing firm, but we feel tired and weary and a little tattered and torn, just like my old bag I used to carry with me on airplanes. Our light just isn't as bright and shiny as it used to be. But Psalm 18:28 says, "*You, O Lord, keep my lamp burning; my God turns my darkness into light*" (NIV 1984).

The most important thing that you need to do to keep your light burning brightly is to come into His Presence. Don't come hurriedly, watching the clock, but wait on Him and invite Him into your presence, saying, "Lord, I come to You. I want Your agenda for my life and I want to be a vessel that will be used in Your kingdom. I need to hear from You today and I need for You to guide my steps." I encourage you to set aside your agenda and concentrate on the agenda of the Lord—seek Him, open your heart to Him, and delight yourself in Him.

PSALM 37:4

4 Delight thyself also in the Lord: and he shall give thee the desires of thine heart.

We need to ask ourselves the question, "Have I been neglecting to delight in the Lord? Have I been neglecting my relationship with my Heavenly Father?"

Asking the "Whatsoevers"

When my children were young, if I needed somebody to take care of them, I was going to choose someone I had a close relationship with, and oftentimes that was my niece Candas. She and I go back a long way—she was the flower girl in my wedding. After I had children, I called upon her to take care of them, knowing that they'd be safe when they were with her. Why? Because I had a close relationship with her. I trusted her. So I felt comfortable in asking her to do something like that for me. I had a trust in her that she could do what I needed her to do.

When we develop that kind of relationship with our Heavenly Father, what does He say?

JOHN 14:13

13 Whatsoever ye shall ask in my name, that will I do, that the Father may be glorified in the Son.

With our natural relationships we're limited many times in what we can ask of someone, but we can have such a strong relationship with God that we can ask Him for the *whatsoevers*. We can enter into His Presence and talk to Him just like we were talking to someone else that we know really well.

We don't have to enter in and say, "Our Heavenly Father, the Lord God of this universe, we come to You ever so humbly, entering into Your Presence, O God."

No, when I go to my Heavenly Father, I'm very direct! First, I say, "Father, I love You. Thank You so much for all that You have done for me. Thank You for Your love, for Your grace, and for Your mercy." Then I say, "Hey, God, I've got a real problem. This is what I need."

Other times I'll say, "God, I don't understand what's happening in my life. I've done this and that, and I'm still not receiving an answer. What am I doing wrong?" I just put it all out before Him because God doesn't mind us asking Him a question if we're doing it respectfully.

If you come into His Presence expecting, He will show Himself mightily to you. As you bask in His Presence, He will change you from being tattered and torn to bright, shiny, and new—no wrinkles, no dirt, and nothing weary or worn or broken!

Have an Ear to Hear

The Lord said in Matthew 11:28 "*Come unto me, all ye that labour and are heavy laden, and I will give you rest.*" When there's no rest, God can't speak to you and you can't listen because you have so much confusion in your spirit. And if you aren't sensitive to the Voice of God, you can miss a good opportunity or miss receiving the answer you need from Him.

I remember the time my husband and I bought a '50s CD through a television advertisement. We grew up enjoying that kind of music, so we thought it would be fun to listen to our old favorites again. We played it while we were eating dinner and at first it was enjoyable. But after listening to that CD for two hours my heart was sick! It wasn't bad music, but I didn't want my mind to be cluttered with things that didn't have anything to do with the Lord. I always try to keep myself built up in the Lord so I can hear His voice!

One thing that I want to get across to you in this chapter is the importance of having an ear to hear. I'm not talking about a natural ear to hear what the world is saying, but a spiritual ear to hear what the Spirit of God is saying in your heart.

When we are faced with disturbing or confusing circumstances, we tend to concentrate on those things so much that we don't listen to the inward man, our spirit man. We're often unable to hear the still, small voice of God in our hearts. Yet, entering into the throne room of God through prayer is where we get new strength, hope, guidance, and direction—a new lease on life!

As you talk to Him like you would anyone you have a close relationship with, the gentle voice of His Spirit will teach and show you things that you need to know. And He will ever so gently prompt you about the things He is leading you to do.

Act on Inner Promptings

We need to begin to pray by the prompting of the Holy Spirit instead of responding to what the enemy is bringing from the outside. What do I mean by that? If the only time that we're driven to our knees (literally, or in our hearts) is when circumstances in our lives cause us to pray, then we are praying defensively. We are praying in an effort to put out all the fires in our lives. Thank God that He is going to be with us and help us put out all of those fires. Yet how much more does He want to help us pray offensively, so we can keep those fires from coming into our lives in the first place!

"*The spirit of man is the candle of the Lord*," King Solomon said in Proverbs 20:27. *Matthew Henry's Commentary* compares our spirits to a candle that God lights, in the sense that "it is the inspiration of the Almighty that gives us understanding."[1] We need to be able to pray with His Spirit leading us through our spirits. That will help us hear His voice so that our spirits will be sensitive to His promptings and alerted of things to come.

JOHN 16:13

13 Howbeit when he, the Spirit of truth, is come, he will guide you into all truth: for he shall not speak of himself; but whatsoever he shall hear, that shall he speak: and he will shew you things to come.

If you'll get your spirit hooked up with the Holy Spirit, He'll give you what I call "prayer impulses." He will show you what God wants to do for you and how the enemy is trying to destroy you. If God wakes you up in the middle of the night to pray, then pray! You may be wondering, *How do I know that it's the Lord waking me up?* If I wake up in the middle of the night, I know I don't ever do that on my own so I know that the Lord is prompting me to pray. And I start praying!

If I think of somebody that I haven't thought of in years, I don't just say, "I wonder how So-and-so's doing? It's been a long time since I thought about them." No, I know the Holy Spirit is trying to alert me to something and He's trying to get me to pray offensively. So I start praying for that person. I may not know what the problem is, but I don't have to know what I'm praying for—I just need to start praying!

Another way you can know that the Lord is trying to prompt you about something is through this kind of thought that comes to you: "I wonder about So-and-so; I just feel impressed that I need to send them some money." It's probably not just a vague thought but the prompting of the Holy Spirit. They may be believing for finances, and you may be the instrument that God wants to use to help them.

So many times we just let those inner promptings pass over us, but it's so important that we do not override what the Lord is saying on the inside of us. He wants us to be sensitive to His promptings because He wants to move through each and every one of us. He wants to alert us, warn us, and show us things to come. So as Christians we need to come to the place where we begin to listen to the Spirit of God on the inside of us—not just for ourselves, but to be a witness for Him and to minister to those who need God's touch.

Go Out and Shine

I remember one fall day when I was able to witness to someone who unexpectedly crossed my path. She was an alcoholic and had tried to quit drinking, but she was still struggling with it. I could have missed the opportunity had I not been sensitive to God's promptings.

I went to grab a quick lunch in a restaurant where she worked, and she came up to me after recognizing me from our television program. I didn't really feel I had time to talk to her because I had a busy schedule that day, but I was polite. She came over to my table three times, and the third time she asked if I could help her. At that point, my spirit was just exploding because I realized that this wasn't just an interruption in my day; it was an assignment from God! Suddenly I forgot about everything else but listening to what the Holy Spirit was telling me about how to minister to her!

There is a world to win for Christ and God has chosen each one of us to be a witness. In Matthew 5:14 it says that we are the light of the world. Jesus came to this world as a gift from God to be the Light of the World, and He wants to shine through us. That was His mission—and it should be ours too. We've got a new light—the light of Jesus on the inside of us—to help us go out and shine, even in the darkest places (vv. 5:14–16).

Begin to pray for opportunities to witness for the Lord and for God to help you become sensitive when He brings an opportunity your way. Remember that it is easy to miss these opportunities by being too busy or distracted to pick up on His signals and promptings in your heart.

Keep the Sparkle!

2 TIMOTHY 1:6 (AMPC)

6 That is why I would remind you to stir up (rekindle the embers of, fan the flame of, and keep burning) the [gracious] gift of God, [the inner fire] that is in you. . . .

Recently I looked up the word *kindle* and found that it means "to stir up, to arouse," and I especially like this meaning—"to shine." Have circumstances come your way and dimmed your light? Does it take you quite awhile to remember the last time that you shined? I hope this chapter has begun to rekindle the light on the inside of you because it's so important that you keep the sparkle, the joy, in your life!

If your light is flickering and about to go out, if you're tired and worn out, check up on the amount of time you're spending with the Lord. He doesn't want you to live with weariness. He doesn't want your life to be dull and dim. He speaks to each of our hearts when we seek Him and gives us the wisdom, strength, and ability to perform our daily tasks as we spend time with Him. (See Isa. 40:31.) So, surround yourself with His Presence and commune with Him, and He will give you a brand-new light. You'll be glowing with His power and anointing and have the fire of the Holy Ghost on your face!

We are living in times in this world that we need to be sensitive to the things of God continually. Right now I encourage you to declare out loud: "Lord, here I am. Take my life. I commit it to You and I commit to do as the Word says—seek first Your kingdom, commune with You, and pray at all times, on all occasions. From this day forward, I'm going to be sensitive to Your Voice. I ask You to lead me, guide me, direct me, show me things to come, and help me fulfill what You have planned for my life." Now I encourage you to go out and be a light to this world!

Chapter 2

A New Toothbrush

Cleaning Up the Words of Your Mouth

EPHESIANS 5:25–26

25 . . . Christ also loved the church, and gave himself for it;

26 That he might sanctify and cleanse it with the washing of water by the word.

Some people just naturally enjoy waking up early, but I'm not one of those people. I'm just not a morning person. My energy level actually increases around midnight! So it could be challenging for me to say anything positive before I get out of bed, especially words of praise and thanksgiving. I'd prefer to say, "Oh, it's morning. I will not rejoice and be glad in it." But I have learned the value of speaking the right kind of words throughout the day, beginning with when I first get up. So even before my feet hit the floor, I start saying Psalm 118:24, "This is the day the Lord has made; I will rejoice and be glad in it," because a lot can happen between the time you sit up in bed and when your feet hit the floor!

One day I was planning to go on a trip out of town for a speaking engagement. When I started to get up out of bed that morning, I didn't realize that for some reason my foot was asleep. So when I put that foot on the ground, it wouldn't hold me up, and I collapsed on the floor with all of my weight on my ankle! I immediately thought that I'd broken my ankle.

The pain was so excruciating that my husband had to pick me up off the floor and carry me because I couldn't walk. He drove me to the doctor, and by the time we got there my ankle was badly swollen. After the doctor examined me, his diagnosis was that I had severely twisted my ankle, tearing all the ligaments in it—and that it would never again be as small as it used to be.

I didn't want my ankle to be big. I'm not a ballplayer, and I didn't want to have the telltale signs of a ballplayer's injuries! As I sat there gripped with pain, it wasn't easy to say, "My ankle will go down, it will be the same size as the other, and I won't have to buy two sizes of shoes." But I said it by faith and went throughout the rest of my day in the strength of the Lord. And no matter how much my ankle hurt, I kept declaring by faith, "This is the day the Lord has made. I will rejoice and be glad in it!"

The swelling in my ankle did go down eventually and that ankle is now the same size as my other ankle. It went down because I know the power of speaking the right words—God's words! I could have said, "Oh my goodness, my ankle's always going to be big!" No, we have to speak to those negative things that try to come into our lives because our words form our world. Speaking the wrong words is like carrying around an old toothbrush in our old, wrinkled bag—that toothbrush represents our mouth and the words that come out of our mouth.

Any dental hygienist will tell you that you're supposed to change your toothbrush every so often. If you've ever tried to use an old toothbrush, you know that a worn-out toothbrush probably won't clean anything!

That old toothbrush represents how we can be so consumed with the negative words that have been coming out of our mouths that we don't even realize our mouths need to be cleaned up! Words of disappointment, words of "I can't make it," "I'm so tired," "I'm so stressed out," "I don't have enough"—all of the negative words that we've spoken—are affecting our lives in the wrong way. Is it time *you* cleaned up your mouth?

Having a good day doesn't just happen. I believe it begins with the words we speak. Words can devastate or edify; they can build up or tear down. Words can motivate us to accomplish an impossible task or cause us to give up in despair. We must be so careful what we say because we are snared by the words of our mouths (Prov. 6:2)! How important are the words we speak? I believe that if I hadn't learned to speak positive, faith-filled words each day, I would have had a very different outcome with my ankle.

We speak a multitude of words daily, but how often do we really pay attention to the words themselves? It's very important to realize that we are creating our world by the words we speak.

So this chapter is designed to build up your confessions and encourage you to make it a practice to only allow yourself to speak faith-building, positive words—words that encourage, heal, build, and cheer up.

Right now take a moment and reflect upon the kind of words you have been allowing yourself to speak. Are they negative or positive words? Are they uplifting words or words of criticism? If things aren't going well for you and you have wondered why, you may find as you read on that you have created your situation by your own words and you need to put a watch over your lips. The good news is that you can change your world by changing your words!

Speak Positive Words

I recently read a book about Mary Kay (founder of the multi-million dollar cosmetics and skin care business) and her leadership styles. One of her policies embodies this message on our words. Every time that someone in her organization would ask, "How are you?" the standard answer was always, "I'm great." When I read that, I thought, *What a wonderful confession!* I don't care what's going on, we can speak positive words and be great in the strength of the Lord.

When it comes to speaking positive, faith-filled words, one Bible character that I often refer to is King David. He was a courageous young man who was great in the strength of the Lord. In 1 Samuel 17, when the giant, Goliath, kept speaking harmful words that put fear into the hearts of the Hebrew army, David said, "*Who is this uncircumcised Philistine that he should defy the armies of the living God?*" (v. 26 AMPC).

When David was brought before King Saul because David wanted to fight Goliath, this godly teenager told the king, "*The Lord Who delivered me out of the paw of the lion and out of the paw of the bear, He will deliver me out of the hand of this Philistine*" (v. 37 AMPC).

Later, when Goliath spoke threatening, negative words to David on the battlefield, David counteracted with words of faith.

1 SAMUEL 17:45–47 (AMPC)

45 You come to me with a sword, a spear, and a javelin, but I come to you in the name of the Lord of hosts, the God of the ranks of Israel, Whom you have defied.

46 This day the Lord will deliver you into my hand, and I will smite you and cut off your head. And I will give the corpses of the army of the Philistines this day to the birds of the air and the wild beasts of the earth, that all the earth may know that there is a God in Israel.

47 And all this assembly shall know that the Lord saves not with sword and spear; for the battle is the Lord's, and He will give you into our hands.

David certainly faced a challenging situation, but he looked on the positive side of it and spoke from his heart. As I'm sure you know, what he said in those verses came to pass!

For years I have endeavored to speak positive words, even though it's not always easy. Often when I am facing a challenging situation, my head wants to say, *This can't be done*, but I don't let myself focus on that thought or feeling. Each time, I allow my heart to speak a confession of faith, saying, "I can do this in the strength of the Lord."

I don't care what may come my way, I don't care what obstacle may block my path—I'm going to choose to speak positive words from my heart and rejoice! When I need to get up in the morning, my body may be a little tired because I may not have had as much sleep as I really needed, but I confess every day, "This is the day that the Lord has made. I choose to rejoice and be glad in it!" Then I speak to my body and say, "You will rejoice! You will have energy! You will do what's necessary today!"

I don't allow the words, "I'm so tired," to come out of my mouth because I know that my world is going to be formed by my words. The more I say I'm tired, the more tired I'm going to get. I've got too much to do to get tired! So I say, "The strength of the Lord dwells in me and I go in His strength. I'm not getting weaker; I am getting stronger. My youth is being renewed by the Lord" (Ps. 103:5). I know this works because my staff members tell me that they have to run to stay up with me—and I'm twice the age of most of them!

So often we wait until difficult circumstances happen in our lives to clean up our mouths. But we need to start speaking positive, faith-filled words now rather than waiting for bad things to happen before we start confessing God's Word.

For instance, don't wait until you start having symptoms of Alzheimer's disease to start confessing that you have a sound mind and a good memory. Every day I say over myself, "I have a good memory. I have a sound mind. I go in the strength of the Lord and continue to have strength. I am going to have strength even when I'm 100 years old!"

I remember hearing my father-in-law, Kenneth E. Hagin, say that there are things that were put in motion in people's lives that could not be changed because they were put in motion years ago. I'm putting in motion positive things in my life. I'm putting in motion that I will live a long time, and not only will I live a long time, but I will live a well, healthy, perfect life, full of strength and with a good memory. I encourage you to do the same. (You can do this for your family too.)

Don't wait until you are older to start confessing the right things. Don't wait another day to start saying, "I have good health. My joints are strong. I'm free from stiffness." No, put those good things in motion now by speaking God's Word!

Don't ever confess, "I'm so tired" or "I'm so broke" or I'm so sick." Don't allow yourself to say the words "I can't" or "This is so hard." Remember, you're going to be snared with the words of your mouth. Instead, make a positive confession: "*I can do all things through Christ who strengthens me*" (Phil. 4:13 NKJV).

Sometimes I don't know how I'm going to do a certain thing, and you may feel that way at times too. Do you know how often the devil tries to say to me, "You can't do that"? When he does, I just declare, "I don't come in my strength, but my help comes from the strength of the Lord!" And if he still keeps hollering, "Oh, you can't do that," I just declare to him, "I can! I can! I can, Mr. Devil, because the Word of God says I can!"

Cleanse Your Heart, Cleanse Your Mouth

You may have noticed by now that our confession of positive words includes scriptures. I like the way Joshua explains it.

JOSHUA 1:8

8 This book of the law [God's Word] shall not depart out of thy mouth; but thou shalt meditate therein day and night, that thou mayest observe to do according to all that is written therein: for then thou shalt make thy way prosperous, and then thou shalt have good success.

In this verse it is obvious that to live a successful, prosperous, abundant life involves the words that come out of our mouths. That alone should motivate us to clean up what we say! According to the Bible, what comes out of our mouths "*comes forth from the heart*" (Matt. 15:18). This is what the Apostle Paul was referring to in the verse I quoted at the beginning of this chapter—"*the washing of water by the word.*" Physical water only cleanses our outward bodies. It takes the Word of God to cleanse our hearts and the words of our mouths.

Living in such a busy world, we often forget the importance of filling ourselves with scripture. In other words, we must meditate on the Word of God! Now, that doesn't mean you can do just a quick, five-minute reading of a psalm every day. Have you ever thought, *I've got to read the Word today; now, let me find the shortest psalm and I will have done my duty*? No, we must take time to read and meditate (think, ponder on) the Word and do that "day and night."

You may be saying, "I don't have any time!" Let me ask you a question. Do you have time to read the newspaper? Do you have time to watch your favorite show on television? Do you have time for your recreational activities? If you have time for those things, you have time to read the Word of God.

How important is it to make time to fill your heart with the Word? There is a real live enemy called Satan, and he is trying to destroy you (see John 10:10). It's the Word going into your heart that's going to come out of your mouth—and that's what will give you strength to overcome any difficulties and challenges that may come your way.

You must be diligent to spend time daily meditating on the Word. As you do, it will become so much a part of you that it will be stronger in you than anything else and you will choose to believe the Word rather than what you see, hear, or feel. Part of believing is speaking, and according to Ephesians 5:25–26 in *The Message*, "*Christ's love makes the church* [that's us!] *whole. His words evoke her beauty. Everything he . . . says is designed to bring the best out of her.*" So when we speak His Word, we are speaking God's best for our lives!

Did you know that you can meditate on the Word even when you're not reading your Bible? I go from one type of meditation to the other. I read my Bible first in the morning, and as I'm getting ready, I turn on Christian music to help me meditate on the Word. When I get in my car, I put on Christian music to listen to while I drive. I'm praising God and meditating on His Word, and that revs me up for the day! I start each morning by building myself up on my holy faith and continuing to do so throughout the day (Jude 1:20). When I return home at night, I play Christian music in my house, and that's how I meditate on the Word day and night.

Being built up through the Word is so important because it's easy to become fearful and distraught these days. Often we're told in the Word, "Fear not." Fear does not come from God; it is a spirit that comes from the devil. The enemy would love for fear to dominate our lives.

When Satan brings fearful thoughts to you, you can combat them by speaking the Word. You can say, "God has not given me the spirit of fear; but of power and love and a sound mind" (2 Tim. 1:7). When fear tries to attack me, I immediately quote Isaiah 26:3, "*Thou wilt keep him in perfect peace, whose mind is stayed on thee: because he trusteth in thee.*"

Perhaps the doctor has given you a gloomy report. You don't have to fear; instead, you can quote Psalm 118:17: "*I shall not die, but live, and declare the works of the Lord.*" If you are going through tough circumstances, look to Isaiah 43:2 for strength and say: "When I pass through these waters, God will be with me; and through the rivers, they shall not overflow me: when I walk through the fire, I shall not be burned; neither shall the flame kindle upon me." When your budget won't balance, quote Philippians 4:19: "But my God shall supply all my need according to His riches in glory by Christ Jesus."

Once you build up your trust in the Lord, fear can no longer dominate you. That's what meditating on and speaking the Word does—it builds up your faith and trust in God. You don't have to fear because you know that He is always there to help when the circumstances of life try to overwhelm you.

Meet the Challenge

You may not be as far along in accomplishing God's plan for your life as you had hoped to be at this point, and you may be wondering why. Let me ask you a question: Have you cleaned up your mouth lately? Are you speaking the right kind of words? Perhaps you have taken the first few steps towards your destiny and then fallen down. You may still be lying on the ground, or you may have decided not to take another step in that direction. I believe that through this book our Heavenly Father is encouraging you to get up and take another step, just as a parent would encourage their child who has fallen down to get up and try again.

Now that you've come to the end of this chapter, you know that as you take each step to fulfill God's plan for your life, you must speak words of faith. You can say something like, "Okay, God, with You I will make it this time." Remember, the devil will try to do a number on you and whisper harmful words in your ear. When he does, just kick him out of your life with the words of your mouth!

As you begin to take the initiative to speak edifying, uplifting words, you will find that you'll start rising to the top. Opportunities will start knocking on your door, and you can take advantage of those opportunities with confidence, knowing that with God's wisdom, strength, and His Word, you can do all things. That's why I love Philippians 4:13 so much—"*I can do all things through Christ which strengtheneth me*." Not only has this verse helped me through various disappointments and difficult circumstances in my life, but it has also helped me to have confidence in my ability through Jesus Christ. I know that I'm not doing anything alone because the Lord strengthens me!

If you will put a watch over the words you speak, it will help you make it through every circumstance of your life! Begin now by simply refusing to focus on the circumstances, grabbing the Lord's hand, and saying, "Father, You said in Your Word that You would never leave me or forsake me. You promised to always be with me. I take Your hand by faith, and I expect You to lead me to victory!"

Chapter 3

A New Fragrance

Living God's Way—the Act of Walking in Love

JOHN 13:34 (NKJV)

34 A new commandment I give to you, that you love one another; as I have loved you, that you also love one another.

A popular passage in Deuteronomy 28 talks about all of our blessings—how we will be blessed in the city, blessed in the field, and the fruit of our body (our children) will be blessed (vv. 1–4). We love to concentrate on verse 13 that says we'll be the head and not the tail and we'll be above and not beneath. While that is all true, sometimes we don't read the rest of verse 13 that gives the condition on which these blessings are based.

DEUTERONOMY 28:13 (AMPC)

13 . . . if you heed the commandments of the Lord your God which I command you this day and are watchful to do them.

You may wonder why sometimes your confessions of faith are not becoming realities. Ask yourself this question: *Am I heeding the commandments of the Lord?*

What has He asked us to do? There are many commandments that we must do, and we must get into the Scriptures to find them and obey them. But in this chapter I want to talk about one specific commandment—the commandment to walk in love.

MATTHEW 22:37–40

37 Jesus said . . . , Thou shalt love the Lord thy God with all thy heart, and with all thy soul, and with all thy mind.

38 This is the first and great commandment.

39 And the second is like unto it, Thou shalt love thy neighbour as thyself.

40 On these two commandments hang all the law and the prophets.

In verse 39, Jesus is talking about the commandment to walk in love. He isn't referring to loving others just in words and thoughts either, but with consistent actions and deeds. Acts of kindness are one of the strongest voices in the love walk. I believe that we've only scratched the surface of this commandment. The fact is if we consistently operate the love commandment, we don't have to worry about the other commandments; they will become second nature to us.

What is supposed to come out of us when we practice the love walk? A new fragrance!

EPHESIANS 5:2

2 Walk in love, as Christ also hath loved us, and hath given himself for us an offering and a sacrifice to God for a sweetsmelling savour.

In this verse, the Apostle Paul used a Greek word for "sweetsmelling savour" that means a *sweet odor* or *fragrance*.[1] I got excited when I found this out because I thought, *When we walk in love, we're supposed to smell like a brand-new bottle of cologne!* Most women carry a certain fragrance of perfume or cologne in their bag. And I believe God wants to give us a new perfume—the fragrance of walking in love!

The cares of life can bring us so far down in our love walk that if there's any fragrance left in us, it comes out of our old, worn-out bag and smells like cheap perfume. In this chapter we're going to check up on our love walk because if we want to live a life of faith, we must remember that faith works by love (Gal. 5:6).

The act of walking in love is a very important part of relationships. If we don't walk in love, then what's the alternative? Life is just too short to be living a life of selfishness and turmoil. We've talked about seeking first the Kingdom of God, but the fact is that when we place God first in our lives, every hostility will evaporate and the love of God will permeate our lives *like a new fragrance*!

Can people around you "smell" the fragrance of God's love flowing through you? You may be thinking, *That's just not my personality type*. In the natural you may not be a person who shows love easily, but the fact is that if you are born again, the love of God has been "shed abroad" in your heart, for God is love (Rom. 5:5; 1 John 4:16). When you seek the Lord and yield to His love in you, it has to come forth. Then, no matter what's going on around you, love will come out of your heart and your mouth.

Practicing the Love Walk

It is important (and scriptural) that we learn to practice love in our life on a daily basis, yet in the times in which we live, many people seem to have lost sight of the importance of walking in love or how to develop a love walk. Second Timothy 3:1–5 sheds some light on why.

2 TIMOTHY 3:1–5 (NKJV)

1 But know this, that in the last days perilous times will come:

2 For men will be lovers of themselves, lovers of money, boasters, proud, blasphemers, disobedient to parents, unthankful, unholy,

3 unloving, unforgiving, slanderers, without self control, brutal, despisers of good,

4 traitors, headstrong, haughty, lovers of pleasure rather than lovers of God,

5 having a form of godliness, but denying its power.

These verses are certainly being fulfilled all around us today. Even Christians can struggle with these issues at times and be hindered from practicing the commandment to walk in love. Many refer to 1 Corinthians 13 as "the love chapter" but they would rather skip over reading that part of the Bible. I admit I have felt that way at times, but the Lord still leads me to read it. I hope that you will do the same because it shows us what it means to practice walking in love.

1 CORINTHIANS 13:4–7 (AMPC)

4 Love . . . is patient and kind.

5 . . . Love (God's love in us) does not insist on its own rights or its own way, for it is not self-seeking; it is not touchy or fretful or resentful; it takes no account of the evil done to it [it pays no attention to a suffered wrong].

6 It does not rejoice at injustice and unrighteousness, but rejoices when right and truth prevail.

7 Love . . . is ever ready to believe the best of every person. . . .

If we would practice this passage daily, we could live peaceful, productive lives. The problem is that our flesh often gets in the way. Instead of ignoring injustices that are done to us, for example, we want to get even; instead of walking in love, we want to repay evil for evil; or we forgive but we don't forget. No, love forgives *and* forgets. Love shows compassion. And love does not gossip!

We must never gossip about others. Have you ever heard the terms *talebearer*, *rumormonger*, or *scandalmonger*? These are other names for a gossip and certainly not good titles to bear. You may be on the phone and the person you're talking to says, "Did you hear what happened to So-and-so? Did you hear what So-and-so did?" Then they go off on a tirade of destructive words about that person. By the time this gossip goes from one "friend" to the next, it's not even close to the truth. On occasion I've had to stop a talebearer in mid-sentence and say that I refuse to listen to anything but uplifting words.

Proverbs 26:22 says, "*The words of a whisperer or slanderer* [a talebearer] *are like dainty morsels or words of sport [to some, but to others are like deadly wounds]; and they go down into the innermost parts of the body [or of the victim's nature]*" (AMPC). According to this verse, spreading gossip is the same as inflicting a deadly wound on the targeted person!

To operate in love means to not judge others. If you were in their shoes, how would you want to be treated? We all need to ask ourselves that question and follow that guideline, and then watch how our attitudes and judgment err on the side of mercy—even with our children. If you were the child and they were the parent, how would you want to be treated? Could you abide by your own rules?

We constantly have to practice our love walk. Sometimes we think we're doing pretty well until something comes along that just throws us a curve. Suddenly we don't want to practice love in that area.

Somebody does something awful to us! Someone talks about us behind our backs! You know, it hurts me when someone talks about me. I love everybody, but when somebody criticizes me, it can make me cry. Then I get mad and I want to say, "Well who are they to judge me?" I have to make a decision to operate in love just the same as anyone else!

The bottom line is that walking in love involves cleaning out all the strife and gossip in your life; cleaning out negative attitudes you may have towards yourself and others;

praying for a love and compassion for others to encompass you; and perhaps most importantly, practicing Mark 11:25, and forgiving others.

Always Walk the High Road

One of the things I witnessed in the life of my father-in-law, Kenneth E. Hagin, was that he not only taught the love walk, but he truly lived it. I don't care what anybody said or did, he never considered getting even. He always operated in love.

I remember times when my husband and I would get exasperated when we heard others criticize and say hurtful things about our family or ministry. Sometimes we expressed our feelings to my father-in-law, but he would tell us, "Don't ever stoop to their level; always walk the high road." I am forever grateful for his example and for him being straightforward with us about these things. After all of these years, I still hear his words ringing in my ears when I'm tempted to walk the low road and stoop to someone else's level to get even.

One of the deadliest traps that the enemy sets for us is to cause us to get offended. It wouldn't hurt so badly if it was a sinner who was offending us, but sometimes it's a Christian—someone we don't expect, someone who is supposed to be practicing love! David wrote about this in the Psalms.

PSALM 55:12–14 (NIV 1984)

12 If an enemy were insulting me, I could endure it; if a foe were raising himself against me, I could hide from him.

13 But it is you, a man like myself, my companion, my close friend,

14 with whom I once enjoyed sweet fellowship as we walked with the throng at the house of God.

Your best friend may offend you, but don't let offense get lodged in your heart. Now, to be honest, being offended is one of the bumps in the road that I have to constantly work on. There are times I just want to dwell on what people did to me instead of forgiving them. My emotions are saying, *Lord, if I have to forgive them, I'm certainly not going to forget what they did!* Yet, if you haven't forgotten, you haven't forgiven.

The most important thing is to practice what my father-in-law constantly practiced—to always walk in love. He was the greatest example of someone who walked down the love path that I've ever seen. He never let anybody offend him. He never took offense at what anyone did. In fact, if you questioned him about it, he'd start quoting his favorite scriptures.

MARK 11:23–24

23 . . . whosoever shall say unto this mountain, Be thou removed, and be thou cast into the sea; and shall not doubt in his heart, but shall believe that those things which he saith shall come to pass; he shall have whatsoever he saith.

24 Therefore . . . What things soever ye desire, when ye pray, believe that ye receive them, and ye shall have them.

I got excited when I heard my father-in-law quote Mark 11:23–24, but then he had to add verses 25–26. What do those verses say?

MARK 11:25–26

25 When ye stand praying, forgive, if ye have ought against any: that your Father also which is in heaven may forgive you your trespasses.

26 But if ye do not forgive, neither will your Father which is in heaven forgive your trespasses.

I'll never forget hearing my father-in-law speak on that subject time and time again. He would say, "Mark 11:23–24 won't work for you unless you practice verses 25–26." I still can hear that in my spirit as plain as day! When he'd say it, I'd straighten up and pray, *Okay God, I know I need my faith to work so I'm going to have to forgive them and forget what they did!*

You simply can't allow offenses to trip you up because faith works by love (Gal. 5:6). So, faith and love go hand in hand.

You will have plenty of opportunities to test this because the test of walking in love is not something you pass one time and never have to experience again. The fact is your love walk will be tested continually. Let's look at one of the greatest examples of that test in the Bible.

Receiving God's Best

In Genesis 12, God told Abraham to leave his homeland and follow Him. Imagine what a traumatic experience it must have been for Abraham to leave the place where he had lived for 75 years of his life—and without

God telling him where He wanted Abraham to go! It was quite a job, but Abraham packed up all of his household and belongings and obeyed the Lord. He took the step by faith and God led him (vv. 1–8).

Did Abraham have tests along the way? Most assuredly yes, just as we will have tests along the way when we determine to walk in obedience to the Lord. One of those tests was when he had trouble with his relative Lot. It began when their servants started fighting with each other. There wasn't enough land for all of their cattle and they started fussing over the land. Abraham certainly realized that this was a problem for both of them and they needed to separate. He said, "Lot, there's not enough land here for both of us. You pick the land you want and I'll take the other land" (Gen. 13:8–9).

What did Lot do? He took what he thought was the choicest land and gave Abraham what seemed to be land that was second rate. But God always knows what the choice land is. Abraham trusted in His God and walked in love, and he was not only called "*the Friend of God*" (James 2:23), but he received God's choicest and best of everything.

You may have been cheated out of something like Abraham was or wronged by a friend or a relative. You may have had terrible things done to you. But God is still looking out for you, and He's going to give you the choice land, if you will just keep a loving attitude.

Sometimes it seems as if I have experienced those kinds of tests on a daily basis! Yet I've always chosen the love walk—and the love walk forgives and forgets and doesn't try to fight back. It makes it so much easier to choose the love walk when we realize that God will defend us and He will give us the victory if we will keep our eyes on Him!

From Ordinary to Extraordinary

1 CORINTHIANS 2:9 (NIV 1984)

9 . . . No eye has seen, no ear has heard, no mind has conceived what God has prepared for those who love him.

Of course, the first person you need to walk in love with is God. (See Matt. 22:37.) The most important thing that you can do is to stay in love with your Heavenly Father, for He has great plans for you. He has great things in store for you. He has a great mission for you to accomplish.

Remember that the enemy would like for us to focus on our "I can'ts." He would like for us to say, "I won't do anything remarkable in life. I won't do anything of any significance. I'm nobody. I'll never fulfill my dreams."

No, you need to begin thinking the thoughts of God. God's thoughts for you are good (Jer. 29:11). He is the master of taking ordinary people and doing extraordinary things with their lives.

Just think of some of the "superstars" in the Bible. David was just a shepherd boy, and he was also the runt of the family. He was out tending the sheep and yet God called him to become king of Israel! David's seven brothers appeared to be better qualified for the job, but God told the prophet Samuel seven times, "No, that's not the one."[2] Finally, Samuel asked Jesse, David's father, "Do you have another son?"

(See 1 Sam. 16:11.) God passed over all of Jesse's sons to select the one who seemed the most unqualified, and yet what mighty things David did for the Lord!

However, David was not without his faults and failures. He messed up significantly at one point in his life, but God still called him a man after His own heart (Acts 13:22). The reason is that David was quick to repent and quick to forgive. Even when somebody was trying to take his life, he never got offended! He always responded in love. (See 1 Sam. 24.)

So many times we want the desires of our heart to be granted, but we stop short of the very thing that will bring those desires to pass—practicing the commandments of walking in love and forgiveness. Often we want forgiveness for ourselves and judgment for everyone else, but we must forgive if we want to receive forgiveness and have our prayers answered. We need to keep our "bottles" filled with love so that everywhere we go, there will be a sweet-smelling savor because we are walking in love.

Yet that is one of the most difficult skills to master, because it's easy to experience such strong, negative emotions towards someone who has hurt you. I've had many opportunities to practice the love walk myself, so I understand that someone might have done something awful to you, something that's very hard to forgive. But I've found that the more you practice love and forgive others, the easier it becomes.

When you walk in love, peace and tranquility will surround you. You'll experience a joy like you've never known before and hatred and bitterness will dissolve away! Your whole life will have a wonderful fragrance—the fragrance of our Lord and Savior, Jesus Christ!

Chapter 4

A New Garment

Putting Into Practice the Power of Praise

ISAIAH 61:3

3 . . . Give unto them . . . the garment of praise for the spirit of heaviness . . . that [the Lord] might be glorified.

One Wednesday night many years ago, I did not want to go to church. I didn't want to smile; I'd had a bad day and I was depressed. I'm not usually depressed, so if *I'm* depressed it's really bad. That night I just wanted to sit at home and do nothing. I didn't tell anybody how I felt because I knew the Word says that we're snared by the words of our mouth (Prov. 12:13), and I had learned to keep my mouth shut when I was having a bad day. But I also knew that "*the thief cometh not, but for to steal, and to kill, and to destroy*" (John 10:10) so I told the enemy, "I'm going to give you a black eye. I'm going to church in spite of how I feel!"

When I arrived at the service that evening, I thought, *Oh God, just don't let anybody smile or talk to me. I want to be left alone!* Later, when the worship service began, it seemed as if every song ministered to my spirit. Soon I joined in praising and worshipping the Lord and my spirit began to be lifted. By the time my husband preached the Word, I was open and receptive to the message and was blessed. When church was over I left rejoicing and strengthened in the Lord.

What happened to me during that service? I changed my garment. I'm not talking about a physical garment. I exchanged that old "spirit of heaviness" that was weighing me down for the garment of praise that the prophet Isaiah described in Isaiah 61:3. Other Bible translations call this garment *"joyous praise"* (CEV), *"a praising heart"* (MSG), and one of my favorites, *"splendid clothes"* (HCSB)! When we don't praise the Lord, it's as if we get out the old baggage again, pull out that worn-out garment of the past—the spirit of heaviness—and put it back on.

When we begin to praise the Lord we exchange our tattered, faded-out garment of heaviness for a brand-new garment, one that sparkles. When you put on that garment, you will shine!

When we put on the garment of praise, the joy of the Lord covers us like splendid, new clothing. It's like wearing a garment that's so new it still has the price tag on it, because we bring praises unto God—and as we come to Him with praise, He gives us joy.

If we're not careful, the circumstances in life can cause us to revert back to that old, wrinkled, tattered garment of heaviness. The Lord may bless us, but in receiving His blessings, we fail to remember the Blesser. We start taking His blessings for granted and forget to thank Him for what He has done for us. Or we begin to have some kind of trouble and we get stressed out or worried about it. Either way, we stop praising God, and before we know it, we've lost our joy.

At those times we need to get down on our knees (either literally, or in our hearts) and have a prayer meeting—just us and the Lord—and we need to start with giving Him praise. We will come out joyful because we will receive into our spirits what I call "spiritual vitamins" that will energize us. We'll have a new spring in our step because we're charged up with the power of God!

Are you tattered and torn and worn out by the cares of this world? Has it been a long time since you expressed your appreciation to the Lord for all that He's done for you? God wants to give you a new garment—the garment of praise—for that heavy spirit!

I made a determination a long time ago that I wasn't going to lose my joy anymore. I'm so stirred up about praising my God that it has to come out or I'm going to burst! If that's the place where you need to be, you'll find out how in this chapter. I'm not only going to share what I've learned about the power of praise, but encourage you to practice being grateful and making praise and thanks to the Lord a part of your life.

We are coming into an era when it's going to take intensity in prayer and reaching the heart of God for us to live victoriously in this world.

How do we do that? We begin by putting on our garment of praise—giving praise and worship to the Lord. Whether we praise God with heartfelt words of thanksgiving or we sing or play worship music, praise is the vehicle that ultimately puts us in touch with our Heavenly Father. There's an old saying that "when the praises go up, the blessings come down." Yet more than that, we enter into the very throne room of God with praise!

Open Up Your Spirit

My husband, Kenneth, and I have a friend named Jimmy. He was a traveling minister who loved to play the tambourine, and he played it very well. When he attended our meetings, he would play his tambourine during the song service, shouting, dancing, and worshipping the Lord with all of his heart.

One time after a meeting, Kenneth said to him, "Jimmy, every time you're in worship, singing and playing that tambourine, you are just so lost in the Spirit. Tell me what you're doing—what's going through your mind at those times?"

Jimmy said, "When I start praising my Heavenly Father and singing those songs of praise to Him, I'm thanking Him for all that He's done for me. I get so excited that I really do get lost in the Spirit. As far as I'm concerned there's nobody there but me and God. And I am praising Him with all of my might!"

Why do most churches play praise and worship music before a time of prayer? People don't respond to silence. Have you ever been in a church service where there was a lack of praise and worship? Did it feel as if the Presence of God was missing? Start singing praises to the Lord and what happens? Whether we sing praises in church, at home, in our cars, or somewhere else, praise music helps us to enter into God's Presence.

When you realize how important praise music is to getting your mind shut off and opening your spirit (your heart) to the things of God, you'll understand why the enemy has tried so hard to pervert music. Satan (who was originally called Lucifer) was in charge of the music in Heaven before he rebelled against the Lord.

So we know that there was an important place in the plan of God for music in our worship.

We need to be aware of Satan's tactics when we are encountering difficult circumstances. He tries to influence us in a variety of ways. One way is through our thoughts. We do not need to entertain his thoughts, because they can keep us from praising God. And praise to God is the key to turning any situation around.

If Satan has come in and endeavored to destroy your life, you can rise above the circumstances by praising God. Begin to praise Him; then watch how things turn around for you. Begin to rejoice even when you don't feel like it. That's when you need to rejoice the most!

Silent Seasons

Have you ever encountered a silent season in your life, a dry season, a season when no matter how much you prayed or read the Bible, it just seemed as if your prayers were getting nowhere? It seemed as though God was so far away. You'd cry out to Him, "Lord, I need to feel Your Presence," but it was as if He was not answering you. I've been there, I know how that feels.

What do you do during those silent seasons? David was someone in the Bible who had a lot of trouble and stress in his life, and he knew about being in a silent season. In fact, he wrote some powerful words about that subject in the Psalms.

PSALM 13:1–3 (NIV 1984)

1 How long, O Lord? Will you forget me forever? How long will you hide your face from me?

2 How long must I wrestle with my thoughts and every day have sorrow in my heart? How long will my enemy triumph over me?

3 Look on me and answer, O Lord my God.

David was expressing his innermost thoughts here, and God doesn't mind us doing that. It's okay to express how we feel to our Heavenly Father. I've said to Him before, "God, this is just not fair!" I've told Him, "God, I've been in this dry season for a long time and I'm tired of being there. I need to see a breakthrough!" Many times David also needed a breakthrough, but how did he get it?

PSALM 13:5–6 (NIV 1984)

5 I trust in your unfailing love; my heart rejoices in your salvation.
6 I will sing to the Lord, for he has been good to me.

David was constantly praising God throughout the Psalms and he was called a man after God's own heart. I believe that we should take a lesson from his habit of praise—and not just when things are going well. During the silent times we need to praise Him! Actually, we minister to Him when we praise Him—and as we minister to the Lord, He will minister to us.

God has great things prepared for every one of us. Our Heavenly Father wants to do more for us than our earthly fathers could ever do. If we're concerned about something, He's concerned about it. He wants us to have the things we need. Whether we receive those things or not depends on whether we fulfill some qualifications. We've already talked about 1 Corinthians 2:9 that says, "*No eye has seen, no ear has heard, no mind has conceived what God has prepared for those who love him*" (NIV 1984). But there's something else I want you to see in this verse. God put a qualifier in it—loving Him.

When your children are little, they may say, "Oh Mommy, Daddy, I love you," but what if after they're grown and they're out of the house, they never call you or come by to see you? What if they never e-mail you or write you a letter? Wouldn't you wonder if they really do love you? When we love somebody, we want to talk to them and be around them.

Now, we say we love the Lord, but I wonder sometimes if He questions how much we really do love Him. How often do we talk to Him? How often do we express our appreciation to Him? Is it only when we need something? Or do we talk to Him and praise Him every day?

The Lord wants you to be grateful for what He does for you. He desires that you thank Him and praise Him. One reason is that when you begin to offer up praise, the joy of the Lord will become your strength (Neh. 8:10)—strength to overcome the troubles, stresses, and silent seasons of life!

A Joyful Way of Life

We have been talking about putting on the garment of praise in this chapter. The garment we had in our old, worn-out baggage was the spirit of heaviness. It was wrinkled and worn-out and dirty because of all the cares of life and the problems that had dragged us down and stolen our energy.

But God has a garment for us that is bright and shiny and new—the garment of praise! When we put on that garment, we begin to get excited about the things of God. So many times we get excited at a ballgame or other sporting events. How much more excited should we get about the Lord, the One Who loves us and saved us with His own precious blood!

Don't let your Christianity become just a way of life. God wants it to be a joyful, exciting experience! He is saying in Isaiah 61:3, "My child, I have given you a new garment, the garment of praise, for the spirit of heaviness. Put on your new garment, and rejoice in Me!"

Conclusion

Many years ago the Lord began dealing with me about the very things I've shared with you in this book. When I finally understood the truths of this message, I was so thankful to get rid of the old baggage in my life and put on all of these brand-new things that God had given me. It made me shout and rejoice in the Lord, and it's been my heart's desire to stir you up in the same way.

I hope this book has stirred you to take what you've learned and practice it daily. If you don't begin to practice these things, the cares of life will set in and you will become tired and forget the great communion that you've been experiencing with the Lord. You'll stop praising Him and that old garment, the spirit of heaviness, will come on you. Then your light will start getting dim again, you won't be standing firm in your faith, you won't know if you can walk in love or not, you'll start saying the wrong words, and you'll live a defeated life.

The next time you are tempted to get all of that old baggage out again, don't do it! Don't dig back in your wrinkled, tattered bag and pull out that worn-out garment. You've exchanged it for the shiny, new garment from the Lord. Live the way He has shown you and you will have joy, power, peace, and an abundant life!

Notes

Chapter 1

[1]Matthew Henry, *Matthew Henry's Commentary on the Whole Bible* (Blue Letter Bible, 1996), Proverbs 20:27, http://www.blueletterbible.org/commentaries/comm_view.cfm?AuthorID=4&contentID=1294&commInfo=5&topic=Proverbs.

Chapter 3

[1]*The KJV New Testament Greek Lexicon* based on *Thayer's Greek-English Lexicon of the New Testament, Smith's Bible Dictionary,* and others (www.biblestudytools.net <http://www.biblestudytools.net>), Ephesians 5:2, "sweet smelling savour," http://www.biblestudytools.net/Lexicons/Greek/grk.cgi?number=2175&version=kjv.

[2]God had sent Samuel to anoint the brother who would replace Saul as the new king of Israel.

Prayer of Salvation
to Receive Jesus as Savior

Dear Heavenly Father,

I come to You in the Name of Jesus.

Your Word says, *"The one who comes to Me I will by no means cast out"* (John 6:37 NKJV). I know You won't cast me out. You take me in, and I thank You for that.

You said in Your Word, *"Whoever calls on the name of the Lord shall be saved"* (Romans 10:13 NKJV). I am calling on Your Name, and I know You have saved me.

You also said, *"If you confess with your mouth the Lord Jesus and believe in your heart that God has raised Him from the dead, you will be saved. For with the heart one believes unto righteousness, and with the mouth confession is made unto salvation"* (Romans 10:9–10 NKJV). I believe in my heart Jesus Christ is the Son of God. I believe He died on the cross and was raised from the dead to pay the penalty for my sins. I confess Him as my Lord.

Because Your Word says that *"with the heart one believes unto righteousness,"*—and I do believe with my heart—I have now become the righteousness of God in Christ (2 Corinthians 5:21). I am now saved!

Thank You, Lord!

Signed ______________________________

Date ________________________________